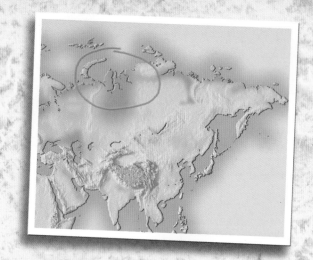

THE MAMMOTH'S TOMB

BY
DOUGAL DIXON

HISTORY HUNTERS

THE
MAMMOTH'S
TOMB

Copyright © ticktock Entertainment Ltd 2003
First published in Great Britain in 2003 by ticktock Media Ltd.,
Unit 2, Orchard Business Centre, North Farm Road, Tunbridge Wells, Kent, TN2 3XF
We would like to thank: David Gillingwater, Dr. Adrian Lister and Elizabeth Wiggans.
Illustrations by John Alston and Simon Mendez
ISBN 1 86007 377 8 HB
ISBN 1 86007 371 9 PB
Printed in Egypt
A CIP catalogue record for this book is available from the British Library.

Would you like to join an expedition to hunt for a frozen mammoth?

The characters accompanying you, Charlie Smith, Dr. Marilyn Petronella, Max J. Heidelmann III and the crew from the Boffinbox Science Channel, are all fictional. But real facts about the work of museums, palaeontologists and scientists have been used to give you an accurate picture of the work they do. The frozen mammoth you will help to discover is also fictional. But its characteristics and the details of its life are based on facts about woolly mammoths.

Interested to know more? Ready to dig for ancient clues?

Then welcome to the City Museum...

CONTENTS

CITY MUSEUM PASS

Name: Dr. Marilyn Petronella
Department: Head of Palaeontology

Interests: Mammoths and dinosaurs, digging and rock-climbing.

CITY MUSEUM PASS

Name: Charlie Smith
Department: Palaeontology – temporary research assistant

Interests: Mammoths and dinosaurs, football and computers.

TEMPORARY

AN EXCITING DAY

Day 1

I've always loved visiting the City Museum with its huge collection of items from across the world. And now, here I am for the holidays helping to sort out the storeroom. I've already come across something very interesting. A few years ago the museum's ethnographer (that's someone who studies different groups of people around the world) led an expedition to Siberia, to study the lives of the Siberian reindeer herders. Amongst the items brought back were a shrivelled-up piece of skin attached to some hair, and a huge tooth. I think they may have come from a mammoth!

Only a few completely frozen mammoths have been found, but I have read that some experts think there might be up to 10 million buried in areas close to the Arctic Circle. The site in Siberia, where the City Museum expedition were working, is in this area. I think we should check this out!

Siberia is the most northern part of the huge Russian Federation.

ARCTIC CIRCLE

NORTH AMERICA

EUROPE

Ural

A woman, from the Siberian Nenet tribe, feeds one of her reindeers. The reindeer antlers are carved into elaborate items.

A traditional Nenet knife carved from reindeer antler. It was collected from herders on the Yamal Peninsula, Siberia.

A mammoth tooth. It is quite small compared with some I have seen in books. Could it be from a young animal?

Hair attached to a piece of skin and bone. Could this really be from a mammoth?

I've marked up a map of Siberia to show where some of the frozen mammoths were found.

Arctic Ocean

Liakhov Islands: frozen mammoth excavated in 1901-1903. It was sent to Paris, the last mammoth to leave Russia permanently.

Kolyma River: Beresovka Mammoth, now in the St. Petersburg Museum, excavated in 1901.

Taimyr Peninsula: a french-led international team extracted a mammoth called the Jarkov mammoth in 1999.

Yamal Peninsula: baby mammoth, nicknamed Mascha, found here in 1988.

Berelekh: baby mammoth, nicknamed Dima, found by gold miners in 1977.

Area where the City Museum mammoth remains were found! A local gold miner told the expedition that both pieces came from a frozen riverbank.

Khatanga: a disused mine, now used as a cold storehouse and centre for the study of frozen mammoths.

Lena River Delta: the first frozen mammoth collected by Mikhail Adams in 1806.

Central Siberian Plain

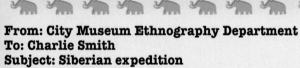

From: City Museum Ethnography Department
To: Charlie Smith
Subject: Siberian expedition

Dear Charlie,

Yes – a few years back some of us from this department went out to Siberia to study the reindeer herders and collect some of their traditional craftwork. Siberia is the northernmost part of the Russian Federation. When it was part of the Soviet Union, during the 20th century, the reindeer herders were persuaded to leave the area where they had traditionally lived, and go to work in cities. But in the early 1990s, after the Soviet Union broke up, they returned to their old way of life. We wanted to see how they were building up their traditions again, a very important part of ethnography work. While we were on the banks of the Yenisei River, a local man gave us the items that you think may be mammoth parts. Show them to Dr. Marilyn Petronella the City Museum's palaeontologist. Since she studies fossils and ancient animals she might be interested. Good luck with your research!

Belts made by the reindeer herders from glass beads.

RESEARCHING MAMMOTHS

Day 2

Dr. Petronella, the City Museum's palaeontologist, is so excited! She didn't know there were any mammoth remains in the museum. She says the mammoth is actually an extinct type of elephant so I've been doing some research, looking at the earliest known elephants through to those alive today. Mammoths lived from about 4 million years ago until just a few thousand years ago. The very last mammoths to exist were a dwarf form. They were discovered in 1992, and their remains were only about 3,700 years old. The dwarf mammoths lived on a place called Wrangel Island, off the north-east coast of Siberia, and were 1.8 metres tall. Small species often evolve on islands to make the best use of limited food. I wonder how big our mammoths were and how long ago they lived?

Dr. Petronella thinks that the tooth came from a young mammoth, but the piece of hair is from an adult. This means there are at least two individuals out there; maybe there could be a whole herd!

A modern-day Indian elephant. Mammoths were more-or-less the same shape as elephants today, but they had sloping backs, curved and twisted tusks and shaggy hair.

The ponies on the Scottish Shetland Islands are a modern example of dwarf animals living on islands.

SHETLAND PONIES

1. MOERITHERIUM

This is the earliest known proboscidean. Moeritherium lived about 50 million years ago, in Eocene times. It was no bigger than a pig and had no tusks or trunk like modern elephants.

2. PHIOMIA

By Oligocene times, 30 million years ago, proboscideans had become larger – 2.5 m high at the shoulder. They were beginning to develop tusks and a trunk to help them feed.

3. GOMPHOTHERIUM

Gomphotherium lived 10 million years ago, in Miocene times. It had tusks in its upper jaw and a pair in its very long lower jaw. It had fewer chewing teeth than its ancestors, but the teeth were larger.

4. DEINOTHERIUM

Deinotherium lived from 10 million to 1 million years ago, during Miocene to Pleistocene times. It had tusks only in its lower jaw and these curved downwards. The tusks were probably used as picks for digging.

...th skulls have fused nostrils at the that look like a single eye socket.

From: The Librarian, City Museum Library and Archive
To: Charlie Smith
Subject: 'Mammoth Legends' by Dr. M. A. Petronella

Dear Charlie,

Below is the paragraph you requested from Marilyn's book. She must be thrilled that there are actually some mammoth remains in the museum!

'Mammoth remains have been known about for centuries, and all sorts of legends have been built up around them. When the ancient Siberians found frozen mammoth carcasses, they assumed that they were some kind of underground animal, like giant moles, that died when they tunnelled to the surface. The bones of mammoths and other ancient elephants were found around the Mediterranean too. Some people thought they had found the bones of giant humans as the skull looks a bit like an enormous human skull with a single eye socket. It is possible that this is what started the ancient Greek legend of the savage, one-eyed giant, the Cyclops.'

THE PAST PRESERVED

Day 3

I'm finding out all sorts of things about frozen mammoths, and I'm presenting my research like they do in the museum displays.

I thought mammoths were preserved frozen in ice, but they were not. They were preserved in frozen mud. Mammoths lived during the Ice Ages (about 1.8 million to 10,000 years ago) when there were cold but dry climates in northern Asia. They lived on open grassland over permafrost (a permanently frozen layer in the soil). Most preserved mammoths that are found come from two periods in time: either before 30,000 years ago or between 13,000 and 10,000 years ago. During these times the climate was slightly milder, and the permafrost became unstable. A mammoth weighing three tonnes could easily sink and get trapped in a thawed-out boggy area of ground. When the bog froze again, the dead mammoth would be preserved, just like in a deep freeze!

1. Mammoths roamed the cold grasslands in herds pulling up low vegetation and grass with their trunks.

Mudflow

Frozen mud

Northern Siberia now consists of tundra (boggy ground with little vegetation). In the mammoths' time it would have been cold grassland.

FROZEN CHICKEN

8

Ice Age Mammoths

2. If the weather became milder, the underlying permafrost would thaw out and form boggy patches where heavy mammoths could get trapped.

3. Once below the surface the mammoth drowned or suffocated. The mud preserved it for a while. Then in winter the mud froze again, freezing the dead mammoth's tissues as well.

4. Over thousands of years the preserved animal would remain undisturbed in the frozen ground.
But if that patch of permafrost became eroded by a stream the dead mammoth would be exposed and would start to decay.

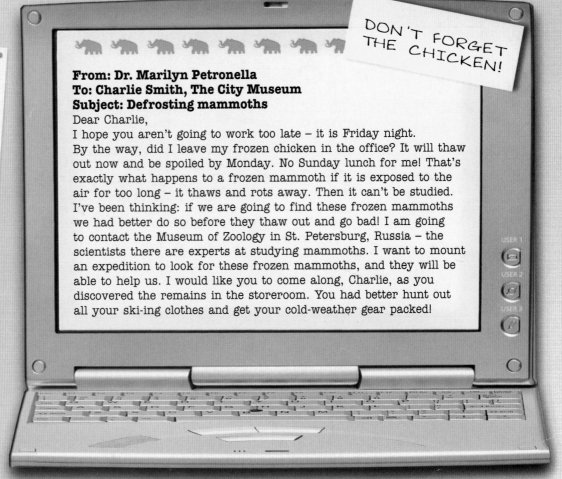

DON'T FORGET THE CHICKEN!

From: Dr. Marilyn Petronella
To: Charlie Smith, The City Museum
Subject: Defrosting mammoths

Dear Charlie,
I hope you aren't going to work too late – it is Friday night.
By the way, did I leave my frozen chicken in the office? It will thaw out now and be spoiled by Monday. No Sunday lunch for me! That's exactly what happens to a frozen mammoth if it is exposed to the air for too long – it thaws and rots away. Then it can't be studied. I've been thinking: if we are going to find these frozen mammoths we had better do so before they thaw out and go bad! I am going to contact the Museum of Zoology in St. Petersburg, Russia – the scientists there are experts at studying mammoths. I want to mount an expedition to look for these frozen mammoths, and they will be able to help us. I would like you to come along, Charlie, as you discovered the remains in the storeroom. You had better hunt out all your ski-ing clothes and get your cold-weather gear packed!

ON OUR WAY

Day 10

I can hardly believe it! Here we are at the Museum of Zoology in St. Petersburg, one of the biggest natural history museums in Russia. St. Petersburg is full of museums and most are to do with history. The city was founded by a Russian leader Peter the Great, and it became the country's capital in 1712. Today the capital city is Moscow. St. Petersburg is Russia's most European-looking city, full of palaces and big houses. Most of these are now museums and art galleries.

The Museum of Zoology is the world headquarters for the study of mammoth remains. Its storerooms contain hundreds of specimens of preserved mammoth bone, chunks of mammoth hair and pieces of soft tissue. The specimens are stored in jars of spirit (liquid with a high alcohol content), to stop them rotting away. The most famous mammoth ever discovered, the Beresovka mammoth, is on display here.

1900: the Beresovka mammoth as it was found emerging from the frozen cliff.

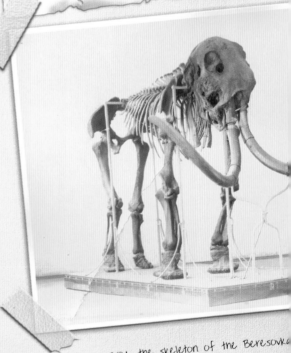

The Beresovka mammoth expedition

MAMMOTH ON DISPLAY 1904

A mammoth is on view in the St.Petersburg Museum of Zoology. The giant animal was discovered by a hunter in a frozen cliff along the Beresovka River in 1900. In 1901 it was excavated by Imperial Academy zoologists Otto Herz and Eugen Pfizenmayer. The expedition cost 16,300 roubles. The body was dissected on the spot, and packed into 27 cases. After a journey of four months – across the frozen landscape by reindeer sleigh, horse sleigh, riverboat and refrigerated train – it arrived at St. Petersburg on 18th February 1902. Tsar Nicholas II, the Russian leader, was delighted, but his wife Alexandra was disgusted by the smell. It has taken two years to prepare the mammoth to go on display.

1904: the skeleton of the Beresovka mammoth goes on display.

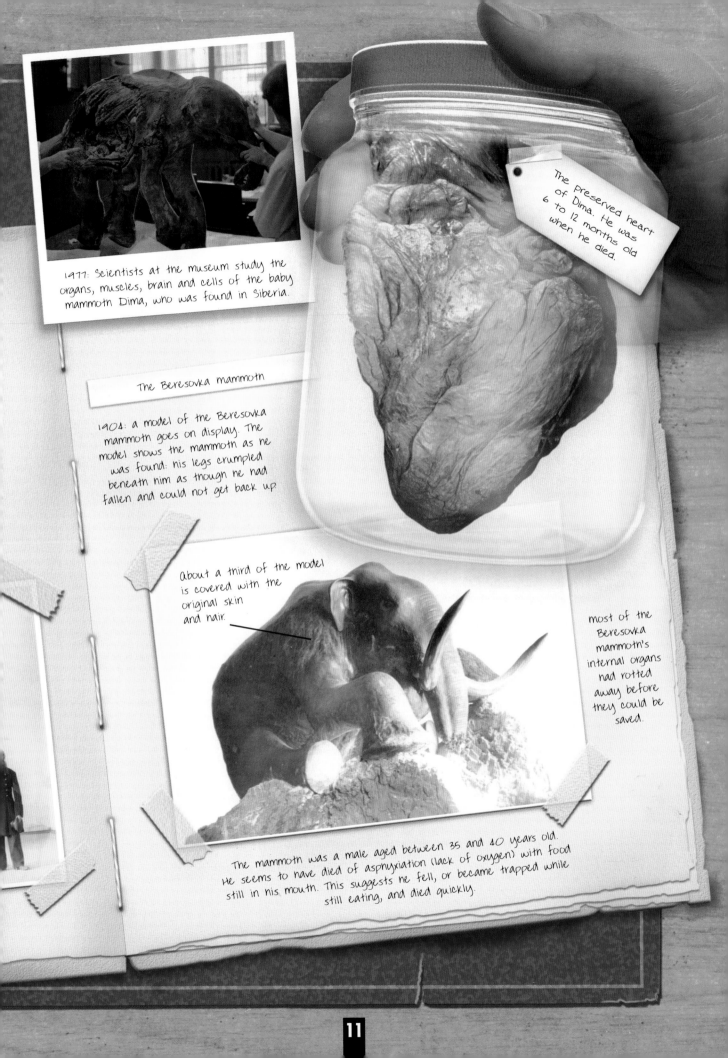

1977: Scientists at the museum study the organs, muscles, brain and cells of the baby mammoth Dima, who was found in Siberia.

The preserved heart of Dima. He was 6 to 12 months old when he died.

The Beresovka mammoth

1904: a model of the Beresovka mammoth goes on display. The model shows the mammoth as he was found: his legs crumpled beneath him as though he had fallen and could not get back up.

About a third of the model is covered with the original skin and hair.

most of the Beresovka mammoth's internal organs had rotted away before they could be saved.

The mammoth was a male aged between 35 and 40 years old. He seems to have died of asphyxiation (lack of oxygen) with food still in his mouth. This suggests he fell, or became trapped while still eating, and died quickly.

A LONG JOURNEY

Day 14

I didn't realise that Russia was so big! Dr. Petronella and I are travelling alone to the area where the bits of mammoth were found, and it is taking days. We have been on a plane, a train and now a river steamer. The first stage of our journey was an Aeroflot flight, an hour and a half, from St. Petersburg to Moscow. Then, after a meal of meatballs and pickled vegetables in Moscow's Yaroslavsky Railway Station, we took a journey eastwards on the Trans-Siberian Railway, to the town of Krasnoyarsk. The train journey took three days across wheat fields and through the Ural mountains. After the mountains came the coniferous forest called 'taiga'.

Now we have begun the last leg of our journey: a 2000 km trip down the Yenisei river.

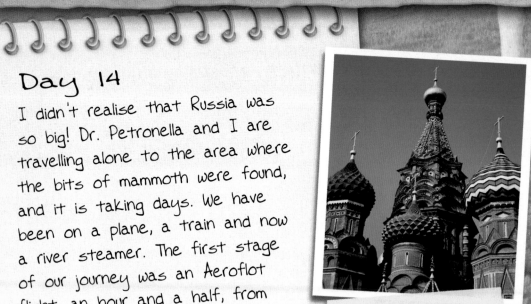

The famous St. Basil's cathedral in Moscow.

The Trans-Siberian railway has the longest stretch of railway track in the world. It takes six days to travel the full length! Here we are pulling into a station en route.

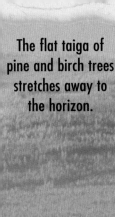

The flat taiga of pine and birch trees stretches away to the horizon.

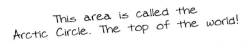
This area is called the Arctic Circle. The top of the world!

Our destination, Dudinka and the mammoth site!

St. Petersburg

Moscow

Five days on the river steamer.

River Yenisei

Krasnoyarsk

Three days on the Trans-Siberian railway.

The Yenisei river steamer. At Krasnoyarsk the river is about 2 km wide. As we sailed downstream it got even wider!

Day 15
We are onboard the Yenisei river steamer heading towards the Arctic Circle.
The Yenisei River cuts Siberia completely in half. Nothing to do but watch the soggy taiga go by.

Meatballs for supper again!

Day 18
We have reached our destination, the small town of Dudinka. We crossed the Arctic Circle two days ago. Now there is just frozen tundra: flat, marshy plains with permanently frozen soil under the surface.

Reindeer herders out on the frozen winter tundra. The sun does not set here. How weird!

THE MAMMOTHS AT LAST

Day 19

We were lucky, as soon as we got off the boat at Dudinka we met a gold miner who remembered the City Museum's expedition five years ago. He was collecting supplies from the boat and agreed to take us to the mining camp. There we met Yuri, the man who had passed the mammoth parts to the team from the City museum.

Yuri was reluctant to talk to us though. He didn't really want to leave his work to take us to the spot where he found the mammoth remains. The gold miners search for tiny pieces of gold in the gravel of the riverbeds; every minute that they are away from the river is lost income for them. Eventually Yuri was persuaded to show us the place where the frozen river bank was being washed away. There, half buried, was the most amazing thing I had ever seen. A thawing and decaying mammoth, but what an unbelievable stink!

The permafrost is a layer of frozen soil beneath the surface. This soil has probably been frozen for 40,000 years.

GPS (Global Positioning System) equipment can be used in remote places to pinpoint an exact location. Satellite signals are then used to find that precise spot again at a later date.

ANIMALS OF THE ARCTIC

Reindeer are the biggest mammals in this part of the Arctic now. In winter reindeer grow shaggy hair and build up layers of fat. This is how the mammoths survived in these same harsh conditions thousands of years ago. The reindeer scrape at the ground to loosen the snow and find the lichen on which they feed. Perhaps the mammoths dug for food in the snow using their tusks?

Yuri a hard-working Siberian gold miner.

Where the river cuts into the permafrost the exposed part of it thaws.

A reddish, fibrous mass of preserved mammoth hair.

Patches of mammoth bone are visible where exposed flesh has thawed and rotted.

A MAMMOTH UNDERTAKING

Two months later

We are back at the City Museum. Dr. Petronella says that in the Arctic Circle there are really only one or two months each year when the weather is good enough for us to carry out our work. She is now convinced that we need a proper expedition to uncover what could be a mammoth herd. But the costs of such an expedition are enormous. The museum cannot afford it so Dr. Petronella says we are going to have to get private investment and corporate sponsorship. That means seeing if any big company will back us. After all, if the expedition is a success it will provide a lot of publicity for that company, something all big organizations want.

Dr. Petronella is also contacting some film companies to see if they would be interested in making a documentary (a factual television programme) about the expedition. I didn't think corporate sponsorship would be anything as exciting as appearing on TV!

marilyn's notes - Expedition Budget	
Food for 20 people for 2 months	£ ??
Cold weather clothing for 20 people	£ ??
Flights, train and river steamer fares	£ ??
Tents and camping equipment	£ ??
Hire of sledges - dog or reindeer?	£ ??
Dog /reindeer food	£ ??
Jackhammers (for breaking the ice)	£ ??
Seismological equipment	£ ??
Trucks to carry the specimens	£ ??
Storage facilities for the frozen specimens.	£ ??
	£ ??

maybe get a grant? Sell my car?
Sell my house? Sell the museum?

BOFFINBOX SCIENCE CHANNEL

Bringing the latest scientific discoveries to the world – as they happen.

Dr. M. Petronella,
C/o City Museum

Dear Dr. Petronella,
We are very interested in your proposed expedition to excavate a frozen mammoth. If you would allow our film crew to accompany you, we would cover the transportation costs for your personnel, storage costs for the specimens and offer you the use of our film crew's helicopter. As you may know, we made a programme about the mammoth site in Hot Springs, South Dakota, USA. The site was discovered in 1974, and 52 skeletons have since been uncovered. The mammoths are the Columbian mammoth — a warm-climate mammoth without hair. We are keen to make a film about your Siberian mammoths as we understand they will be excavated with actual flesh and hair intact!

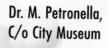

The film crew will include a cameraman, a sound person and an interviewer.

MORE MAMMOTH RESEARCH

This lucky group of scientists is working at the Hot Springs site in South Dakota, USA. These mammoths were the American species, called the Columbian mammoth.

Study of the site has shown that the mammoths must have found a spring at the bottom of a deep hole. They waded into the water to drink, but the sides of the hole were too steep for them to get back out, and they became trapped!

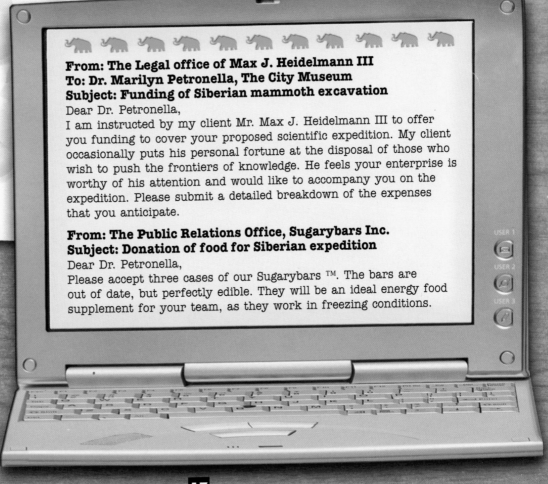

From: The Legal office of Max J. Heidelmann III
To: Dr. Marilyn Petronella, The City Museum
Subject: Funding of Siberian mammoth excavation

Dear Dr. Petronella,
I am instructed by my client Mr. Max J. Heidelmann III to offer you funding to cover your proposed scientific expedition. My client occasionally puts his personal fortune at the disposal of those who wish to push the frontiers of knowledge. He feels your enterprise is worthy of his attention and would like to accompany you on the expedition. Please submit a detailed breakdown of the expenses that you anticipate.

From: The Public Relations Office, Sugarybars Inc.
Subject: Donation of food for Siberian expedition

Dear Dr. Petronella,
Please accept three cases of our Sugarybars ™. The bars are out of date, but perfectly edible. They will be an ideal energy food supplement for your team, as they work in freezing conditions.

USER 1

USER 2

USER 3

BACK TO SIBERIA

At the dig

It's almost a year since we were last here, and now it is the beginning of the summer. Last time it took us days to reach this spot. But now we are using a helicopter, courtesy of Boffinbox TV (I have been told to say this at every opportunity), and we can get to the site quickly. There's a team of volunteers, Mr. Heidelmann III, the TV crew, Dr. Petronella and me! Word has spread about our discovery, and lots of local people are here too. The local reindeer herders are very superstitious; they believe that if you dig up a mammoth you will die.

Some ivory hunters have come out from the cities as well. Mammoth ivory is in great demand since the use of elephant ivory was banned in 1989, and a mammoth tusk is a valuable prize. Some of the tusks we saw last season have already disappeared. Using water from the river, the ivory hunters use high-pressure hoses to thaw out the permafrost. This frees the ivory, but also destroys the mammoth corpses. How can we stop the ivory hunters from destroying our mammoths?

On the local market, mammoth ivory can be sold for two hundred US dollars per kilo.

Ivory carvings for the tourist market are an important source of income. Mammoth ivory is honey-coloured, unlike elephant ivory which is white.

Here I am wrapped up warm in lots of windproof and waterproof layers.

One of the young reindeer herders. He is wrapped up warm in reindeer skins.

EARLY MAN & THE MAMMOTH

A Palaeolithic hut found in the Ukraine.

The mammoth was a great resource to Palaeolithic humans who lived 45,000 – 10,000 years ago. Mammoths were trapped for their meat, skin, tusks and bones. The shape and sturdiness of tusks made them ideal for building the curved walls of huts. This hut has mammoth skulls, with a tusk in each, to form the entrance, shoulder blades and limb bones around the base and a roof made of curved mammoth ribs. The hut was covered in mammoth skins.

The longest tusk ever recorded was 4.2 m long. An average male mammoth had tusks about 2.5 m long.

Day 2 of the dig

I thought that we would have trouble with the ivory hunters, but we've been able to negotiate with them. They've agreed to let us have one good mammoth specimen, and they will take what we leave behind. We gave them some of our petrol for their lorries, and a box of the Sugarybars too; a real luxury for these guys, and we were already getting fed-up eating them!

Our plan is to study as much as we can at the site and collect plenty of samples of the frozen mud to take away with us. The mud should contain remains of the plants that existed at the same time as our mammoth. These remains will tell us a lot about the mammoth's environment. The carcass still has a lot of flesh and internal organs, and we should be able to find out from these how the mammoth lived. The flesh looks horrible and brown once it is thawed. The cameraman bet me that he could eat some. He took a nibble, but spluttered and spat it out. He threw it to our team of huskies, but it was too bad even for them to eat!

SEISMIC READINGS REPORT

We can see what is in the ground using seismic equipment (like scientists use for detecting earthquakes). We hit the ground with a hammer to send a shock wave through the ground then detect the echoes with microphones. The computer readout of the echoes can be analysed by a seismic ex Apparently the survey suggests that there are a few mammoths buried in the frozen bank of the stream, a least one good one.

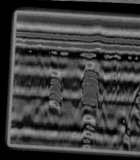

SUGARY BARS

Huskies are perfectly adapted to life in this environment.
Their protective double coat has an outer layer of smooth
hairs and a thick woolly undercoat. Working as a team
they can pull a loaded sled for long distances.

From: Charlie Smith
To: The Palaeontology Department, The City Museum
Subject: Expedition report

Hi to everyone,
Today we have been collecting more samples. When we get back to a laboratory, we are going to use a scientific dating technique called electron spin resonance (ESR) dating which we hope will tell us how long the mammoths have been buried in the mud. The fossilised carcasses will have received a steady dose of natural radiation from the soil surrounding them for the whole time they have been buried. This radiation becomes trapped in the fossils, in the form of electrons (minute particles that carry a negative electrical charge). We measure the amount of radiation coming from the mud, and then measure how much radiation has built up in the fossils. From this we can work out how long the fossils have been absorbing radiation, and therefore how long they have been in the ground.

Next we are going to try to move one mammoth to the mammoth study centre, set up by the Russian authorities at Khatanga.

USER 1

USER 2

USER 3

A FLYING MAMMOTH

Two weeks later

We did it! We extracted an almost complete frozen mammoth in a block of permafrost. It will be transported by helicopter to the frozen laboratory in Khatanga, 600 km away. The block weighed nearly 20 tonnes! We are forbidden by the Russian authorities to take the mammoth out of the country so we will have to study it here.

We waited until September to start the excavation (so that the summer temperatures would not thaw out the body), but it has still been bitterly cold for working. Using a compressed-air jackhammer, we dug out the concrete-hard block of permafrost. Then we used picks and shovels to chip away at each side of the block, until the mammoth's hair began to show. Finally we put a steel frame beneath the block to support it. The excavation took two weeks. The local reindeer herders were very superstitious and wanted us to appease the spirits by sacrificing a reindeer, but were satisfied when we threw some coins into the hole where the mammoth had been.

The last team to fly a frozen mammoth to Khatanga by helicopter stuck a pair of tusks on it. It looked spectacular for the TV cameras, but was not very scientific and a bit dangerous!

MAMMOTH GRAVEYARD FOUND

The skeletons of 156 individual mammoths, between 12,240 and 13,700 years old, have been found in the banks of the Berelekh River in Siberia. Since their discovery in 1970, scientists have been collecting the bones from the permanently frozen soil by thawing them out with hoses.

If we were only collecting bones, we could have used hoses too. However we need to keep our specimen frozen to preserve the soft tissues.

MAMMOTHS MIGHT FLY

OCTOBER 1999

Mammoth hunters in Siberia have just managed to transport a frozen mammoth from its icy tomb to a laboratory by using a helicopter. Crowds stood by amazed as the frozen block containing the Jarkov mammoth, complete with tusks sticking out, landed at the airfield of the small Arctic town of Khatanga.

From: The Cryogenics Laboratory
To: Max J. Heidelmann c/o Charlie Smith
Dear Max,
The cryogenic equipment is ready. Bring whatever samples you can extract from the frozen mammoth. We shall try to find the complete DNA that will be necessary for you to begin the experiments to clone the mammoth.

From: Charlie Smith
To: Dr. Marilyn Petronella
Dear Dr. Petronella,
Take a look at the email that has just come in on my machine for Mr. Heidelmann! DNA? Cloning? I'm not sure I understand all this. I know they used DNA to clone dinosaurs in the book and film 'Jurassic Park'. But what is DNA exactly? Could Mr. Heidelmann actually recreate an extinct animal? What should we do?

Scientist at work!

When Dr. Petronella found out that Mr. Heidelmann's real reason for accompanying us was to try to clone a mammoth, I thought she would be furious. In fact she is just amused. Dr. Petronella doesn't believe it will ever happen, but she regards Mr. Heidelmann's plan as a legitimate scientific project. She is just grateful that he came up with the money to help make the expedition possible.

We are now studying the mammoth in detail. The Khatanga study centre is a disused nickel mine, deep in the frozen rocks. It has become a refrigerated storeroom for thousands of frozen mammoth parts and tusks. The temperature inside is -10°c, the same sort of temperature as out on the exposed tundra. Nothing thaws out until we really want it to.

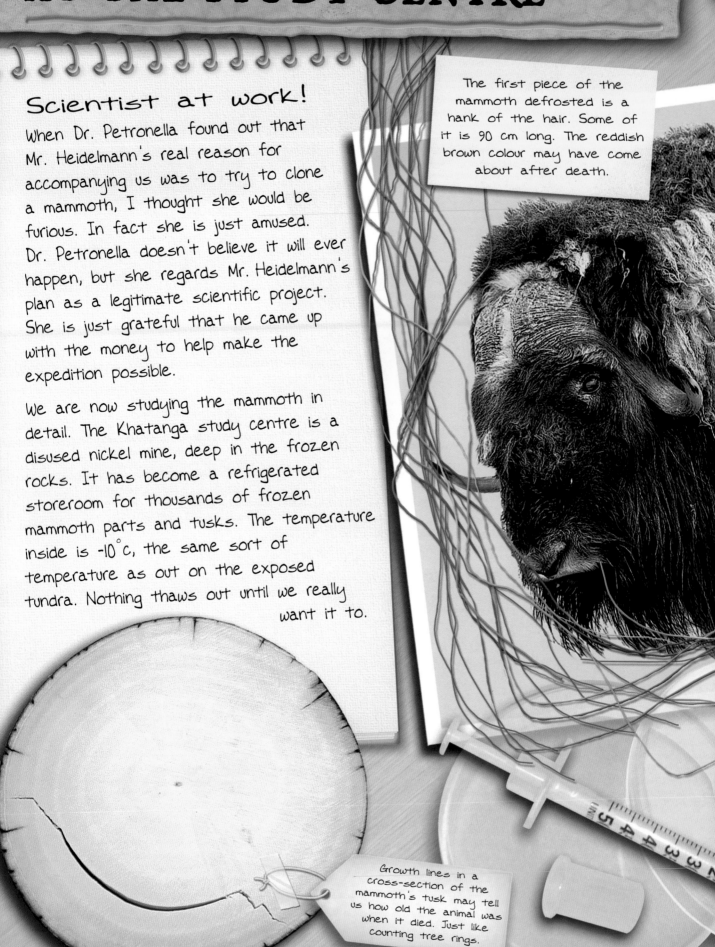

The first piece of the mammoth defrosted is a hank of the hair. Some of it is 90 cm long. The reddish brown colour may have come about after death.

Growth lines in a cross-section of the mammoth's tusk may tell us how old the animal was when it died. Just like counting tree rings.

Using an ordinary hairdryer we can defrost our mammoth bit by bit, like this chunk of flesh. We can then study it a piece at a time.

When handling the frozen remains the scientists have to wear sterile anti-contamination suits, gloves and masks over their cold weather gear. They must not contaminate the mammoth specimens.

Dr. Petronella says that the living mammoth might have been black, like the modern musk ox. Close chemical study of the hair may eventually tell us.

DNA (deoxyribonucleic acid) AND CLONING
FREQUENTLY ASKED QUESTIONS

What is DNA?
All living things are made from cells. Inside the cell is a nucleus – the control centre. Inside the nucleus are the genes – the instructions for making that animal, plant or person. These instructions are stored as a substance called DNA.

What is cloning?
Cloning is the artificial creation of an animal or person that will be identical to its parent.

Could an extinct animal like a mammoth be cloned?
One way would be to remove the egg cell from the womb of a modern, female Indian elephant, and destroy the cell's nucleus. Then a complete and undamaged nucleus from a frozen mammoth cell, containing mammoth DNA (instructions for the cells to grow into a mammoth), would be injected into the elephant's egg cell.
This would then be put back in the elephant's womb. Later, the elephant would give birth to a mammoth.

If DNA is found it may be able to tell us about the health of the mammoth and its relationship to modern-day elephants.

It can't work! DNA begins to deteriorate immediately after death. It would not be good enough quality to create a baby. Anyway, we can let Mr. Heidelmann have his specimens. Some day scientists might get it right!

marilyn P

Back home

Although we could not remove the whole mammoth from Russia, we were allowed to bring back many of our samples to the City Museum. It's amazing just how much information we are able to find out from individual bits of the body, and the mud in which the mammoth was buried. We can tell from the shape of the pelvis that our mammoth was a male. The state of the molar tooth and the rings in the tusk show that he was elderly, maybe 40 years old. Mammoths could live to about 60 years old.

We sawed open his tooth to get at the undisturbed enamel deep inside, and were able to measure the amount of natural radiation it had absorbed, during the time it lay in its tomb. Comparing that with the natural radiation that we measured at the site, we worked out that our mammoth died about 12,000 years ago. If we want further evidence of what our mammoth looked like we can even refer to eyewitness accounts. Our final clues are in France.

Like modern elephants, mammoths went through six sets of molars in their lifetime. The Khatanga scientists say this tooth is probably from his final set.

The mammoth's last meal
Report from
The City Museum Botany Department

Pollen and spores from the mammoth's stomach contents and the mud it was buried in are so distinctive that the species of plants can be identified. The stomach contents consisted of sedges, mosses, grasses and dwarf willow. So the mammoth lived on open grasslands.

Magnified pollen spores

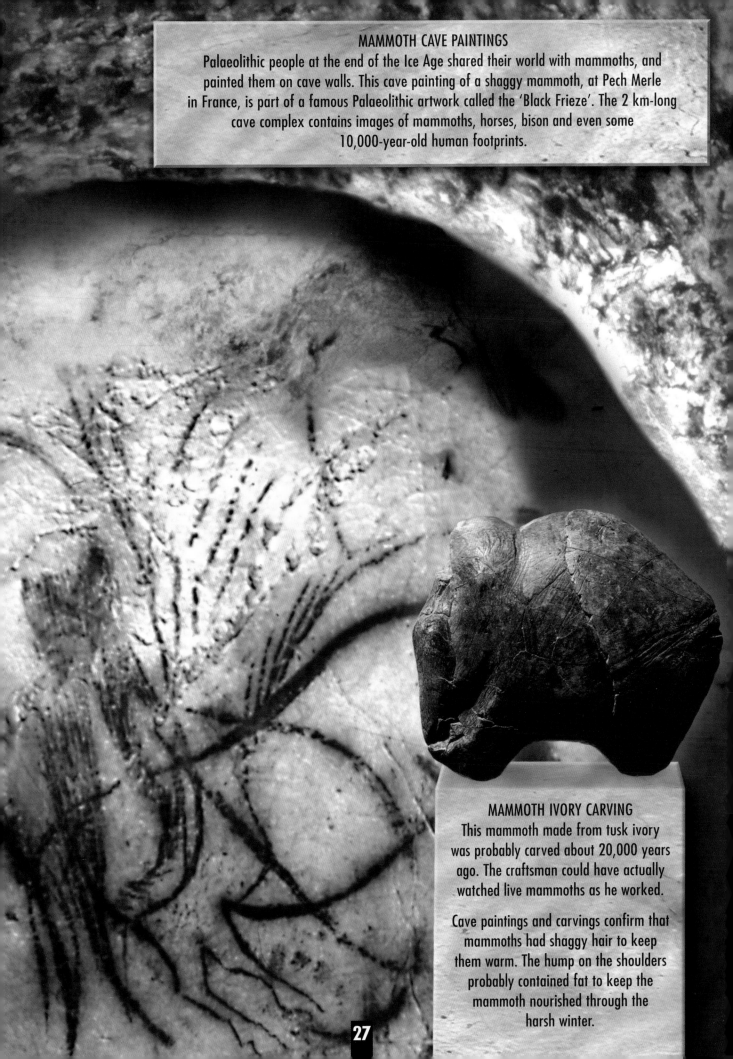

MAMMOTH CAVE PAINTINGS

Palaeolithic people at the end of the Ice Age shared their world with mammoths, and painted them on cave walls. This cave painting of a shaggy mammoth, at Pech Merle in France, is part of a famous Palaeolithic artwork called the 'Black Frieze'. The 2 km-long cave complex contains images of mammoths, horses, bison and even some 10,000-year-old human footprints.

MAMMOTH IVORY CARVING

This mammoth made from tusk ivory was probably carved about 20,000 years ago. The craftsman could have actually watched live mammoths as he worked.

Cave paintings and carvings confirm that mammoths had shaggy hair to keep them warm. The hump on the shoulders probably contained fat to keep the mammoth nourished through the harsh winter.

THE CITY MUSEUM MAMMOTH

Opening day

At last we are able to present our mammoth to the City Museum visitors. The centrepiece of the display is a magnificent animatronic replica of the mammoth itself. We took precise measurements of the skeleton, back in Khatanga, and estimated the volume of muscle that the mammoth had in life. Then this accurate, full-sized fibreglass replica was built. The parts of the pelt (hair-covered skin) that we could bring back are attached to the model, and the rest of the coat is recreated from nylon fibres. The tusks are lightweight plastic, based on the measurements of the originals. We have also been able to display the teeth, the stomach contents and some of the internal organs that we were allowed to bring back. It is important that visitors get to see the original material, and that it is also kept available for scientific research. The expedition has increased our knowledge and understanding of mammoths that little bit more!

Here I am visiting our mammoth at the animatronics workshop. The mammoth will be able to move his head from side to side and reach out to the crowds with his huge trunk. Inside the body a central computer and lots of complicated electronics will control his movements. It would have been amazing to clone a mammoth and bring it back to life, but at least now I can visit the City Museum and see my very own Ice Age giant in action!

THE CITY MUSEUM MAMMOTH

This display sponsored by Boffinbox Science Channel and Max J. Heidelmann III

GLOSSARY

Animatronic A model or puppet that is made to move electronically.

Arctic Circle The imaginary line that surrounds the area in the far north. At some times of the year the sun doesn't rise at all here, and at others it doesn't set.

Carcass The dead body of an animal.

Cell The smallest structural unit of all living matter: plants, animals and humans.

Climate The average weather conditions in a region over a period of years, including temperature and amount of rainfall.

Clone To produce a new plant, animal or human that is identical to its parent.

Coniferous A tree with needles or cones. It usually remains green all year round.

Decay To rot or decompose because of the action of bacteria or fungi.

DNA (Deoxyribonucleic acid) The long-stranded molecule found within the nucleus of a living cell. The pattern of links in the strand of DNA forms the genes.

Dwarf An animal or plant that is much smaller than normal size.

Electron Spin Resonance dating (ESR) A method of dating materials like fossils, bones or even teeth. Over time buried specimens absorb radiation from the soil around them. This is measured, along with the amount of radiation in the soil. These measurements can then be used to calculate how long the specimen has been buried.

Environment The places in which humans, plants and animals live and the external factors such as weather that affect them.

Eocene A part of the Tertiary period of geological time, stretching from 55 to 35 million years ago.

Eroded Being worn away by the wind or by water.

Ethnographer A person who studies people and their cultures.

Evolve To change and develop over a period of time.

Excavate The process by which the earth is dug up and removed in the search for fossils.

Extinct No longer existing as a species.

Fossil The remains of a once living thing, an animal, a plant or even a footprint, preserved in the rock.

Gene Part of the cell of a living thing that determines what that living thing will be like when it grows. An instruction for the development of a particular feature.

Glacier A large mass of ice that moves slowly down a valley or across a continent, melting at one end and replenished by snow at the other.

Ice Age A period of time when climates were much colder than they are now and glaciers spread over large areas.

Jackhammer A large

mechanical drill that is normally used for breaking up road surfaces.

Lichen A plant-like partnership between a fungus and an algae. Lichen can grow on all sorts of bare surfaces like rock or tree trunks.

Miocene A part of the Tertiary period of geological time, stretching from 23 to 5 million years ago.

Molar A grinding tooth at the back of the jaw.

Nucleus The central part of a living cell, containing all the genes (DNA) needed for reproduction and growth.

Palaeolithic Of the earliest part of the Stone Age, from about 750,000 to 15,000 years ago.

Palaeontologist Someone who studies fossils to find out about animals and plants that lived in prehistoric times.

Permafrost A layer of permanently frozen soil found beneath the surface of many cold areas.

Pleistocene A part of the Quaternary period of geological time, stretching from 1.8 million to 10,000 years ago.

Pollen The particles of dust that the male part of a flower releases to fertilize the female part.

Quaternary A period of geological time lasting from about 1.8 million years ago to the present day. It was marked by the appearance of the first humans.

Oligocene A part of the Tertiary period of geological time, stretching from 35 to 23 million years ago.

Radiation Energy radiated in the form of waves or particles.

Replica An accurate reproduction, copy or model of something.

Seismic (equipment) To do with vibrations and movements in the earth.

Species A particular kind of animal or plant.

Specimen A sample of something used for scientific study.

Spore The tiny part of a plant that takes part in fertilization. A pollen grain is a kind of spore.

Taiga The vast stretch of coniferous forest that reaches across northern Asia close to the Arctic circle.

Tertiary A period of geological time lasting from about 65 to 1.8 million years ago. It was marked by the dominance of mammals and the evolution of modern plants.

Tissue The substance from which the parts of a living thing are made. Skin and muscle are tissues.

Tundra A boggy landscape of low-growing plants and lakes that forms over permafrost.

Zoology The study of animals and their lives.

INDEX

t=top, b=bottom, c=centre, l=left, r=right, OFC=outside front cover, OBC=outside back cover

Agence France Presse: 22b. Alamy images: 3br, 3bl, 4cr, 4br, 6tr, 8bl, 12-13, 12tr, 13br, 14b, 15tr, 15c,19tr, 20-21c, 21tr, 23c. John Alston: 7tr, 7cr, 7cl, 7tl, 8cr. Ancient Art & Architecture Collection Ltd 27. Corbis: 4bc, 7bl, 11tl, 12br, 13cr, 14-15c, 16-17c, 17tr, 27br, 29. Natural History Museum: 15br. Science Photo Library: 4bl, 11tr, 18b, 19c. Simon Mendez: 8tr, 9tl, 9tr. Topham Picturepoint: 23tl. Torquay Museum: 10tr, 10br, 11b.